A SPAN BETWEEN THE MOON AND ME

DR AZADEH NEMATI

Belfast
LAPWING

First Published by Lapwing Publications
c/o 1, Ballysillan Drive
Belfast BT14 8HQ
lapwing.poetry@ntlworld.com
http://www.freewebs.com/lapwingpoetry/

Since before 1632
The Greig Sept. of the MacGregor Clan
Has been printing and binding books

All Lapwing Publications are
Printed and Hand-bound in Belfast
Set in Aldine 721 BT at the Winepress

ISBN-13: 978-1907276453 (Lapwing Publications)
ISBN-10: 1907276459

:

CONTENTS

ACKNOWLEDGEMENTS

The world is not as big as we imagine. Sometimes, a glance can change our life and I experienced this. I was full but unable to write. A sparkle flamed this longing in me and I am happy for that. If you burn inside you can create.

Life is very unpredictable. I met an Irish poet at a poetry Festival in India, and I wished we could make friends. Then, I showed my poems written in my silence to her. Hence, first of all I should express my sense of gratitude to Helen Soraghan Dwyer who introduced Lapwing Publications to me as a window to reach my dreams.

Then, I would like to thank Dennis Greig, the patient and knowledgeable editor of Lapwing, who always answered me line by line. It was a distant dream to see my book in my hand in day and read it at nights. Now, it is possible by this, a great man whom I have never met (maybe in past life I met!) but his manifesto is "liberty, equality, fraternity". Thank God that our path had crossed roads.

When we stand like trees possibly all the days are the same but if we flow like a river we will meet more stars. I am appreciative to all those stars in the sky of my life that inspired me and showed me the way in the darkness of night.

May God help me to whisper as far as I am alive then, others sing my songs.

FOREWORD

It is naturally expected that poets write in their first language and take that literary step back into the language and cultural traditions of their own language group and region.

Azadeh Nemati is another Lapwing poet for whom English is not their mother-tongue but write their poems in English. Ulli Gerbig the German poet and Jan Oskar Hansen the Norwegian being two others. In so doing, there is possibly an escape from the tyranny of tradition even if that means adopting the traditions of another language-culture.

Then again. What is the language of poetry that evidentially transcends the limitations of any single spoken or written language?

Azadeh, which in Farsi means 'freedom' has found a freedom in English, not to write what she wants to write but in a manner of writing that is not expected.

Her writing aspires towards an unwritten future from a point in the ever-present present of the human essence. As Pope put it:

> 'Hope springs eternal in the human breast,
> man never is, but always to be blest.'

'Never' but 'to be'. Where do all poets begin? Unconsciously it is probably with an undefined hope, something no more definable than to 'simply be'.

In the saddest and happiest moments in these poems, Azadeh is simply 'being' and that being reaches out to everyone on this planet and celebrates the totality of human existence.

Dennis Greig

A SPAN BETWEEN THE MOON AND ME

DR AZADEH NEMATI

Dedicated to the moon who is always my close friend

MOON

I was swimming in my dreams,

reviewing from the past,

wandering to the future.

In that darkness

I was not aware that the moon,

behind the window,

was gazing at me

at the bright pearls on my face.

I woke up, closed the window.

The moon stayed outside alone.

Oh, God, so sorry for sending her out,

you must be the only witness to my tears!

FLY

To reap the sun,

you need to pass the darkness.

The way of spring

is from the winter.

Waiting to see the butterfly,

take me to your home,

call me, call me, where there is no sound.

Your sound is my lullaby

impetus for metamorphosis

of my inner caterpillar.

Call me, let me rise.

I want to fly, to reach the sky

I am bored on earth.

I need you, call me.

EARTH NO MORE

Every moment,

I am going to the sky

to see the moon and touch the stars.

Every single moment

I am full of deep ocean,

depth of the jungle.

I don't want to be on the surface,

surface of the earth.

Deep, deep in the ocean,

in the jungle, in the sky,

but not on earth.

YOU WENT

You went without farewell

to the waves, to the deep ocean,

you went with the breeze to the top mountain.

Your name went in memories:

among my note-booked leaves

my pencil wrote your name years of times.

You went hand in hand

in our history.

I wonder if spring comes,

will you return, any spring, any autumn?

I don't know if the wave

comes back to the beach,

any wave, any beach

you will return.

I know you went in my notebook,

my tears added to the sea,

sighs to the mountain breeze,

my leadened leaves too pencil heavy.

LET ME IMAGINE

Let me imagine that,

you are still with me,

are you my shadow

walking with me?

Let me imagine that,

you are still my sun

warming me,

you are my star

leading me.

Let me imagine that,

my face is still rainy,

on your shoulder,

my hand is in your hand

to keep me alive.

Let me imagine that

you are still with me

today, yesterday, forever.

CANDLE

I am standing candle-straight,

to burn to the end, but not bend.

I have learnt to burn myself first,

then the butterfly.

I am standing candle-straight,

to make a bright halo around myself

but not dark.

My flame will go with the blow,

but not me.

I am a candle,

I will burn to the end, but not bend.

FLOWER

Be my flower

I want to sniff you,

Fondle your tender petals.

Be my white rose

plain, no other colours.

I will water you every sunshine.

When the sunset arrives

and you wither,

I will die before you, for you.

Our life is so brief,

be my flower

my white rose

the only rose without thorn.

BEE

You are my flower,

I am your bee.

You feed me with your honey

I am your bee.

You don't move

I am my own ragged dance around you.

You are my flower,

I am your small bee.

Cuddle me in your tender petals

tighten them and make a shelter,

I want to be your sweet heart.

SEA IS ALIVE

The sky full of bright dots,

an old bench near the sea,

the romance of sand and sound.

The sea is alive,

never sleeps.

The waves' sound roars along the coast,

gives me freely,

happiness and tranquility,

joy and refreshment.

Oh my sea-live life!

No one could give me those freely.

BEAUTIFUL LAKE

Every day I meet you,

see your beauty,

your calmness,

your fulness, your hidden desires.

Every evening I come to see you,

see the sunset on your wet eyes,

the full moon on your darkness.

Every evening your beauty is my host,

your silence is my lullaby,

darkness my brightness.

You and me,

me and you,

on the old bench,

deep-littered by dry leaves,

under the fingers of bamboo.

Every evening, I am your guest,

you are always kind and accept

my smiles, my tears, my happiness, my sorrow.

Oh beautiful lake, you are my healing.

IF RAIN

Small rain drops down

from the eyes of heaven:

touch the lake

scribble the picture of trees

asleep in rows upon the lake's surface.

Small drops of me rain down

to wash my eyes

and no one knows

if they are

drops of tears or

drops of rain,

on my cheeks

under this rainstorm.

A MISTY ROAD

I will go on a misty road,

in a foggy day,

under the rain,

along a leaf-full path.

I don't know where:

with only my backpack,

I will go, go, go,

so, one day,

I will rise, rise, rise

a black ocean,

welling and swelling,

at day break,

beset by mist,

under the rain…

BLUE HEART

You are in my vicinity,

you are in me

in my deep-rooted desire,

on the intensified sky,

in the shortness of my love,

on the length of a heavy heart.

I am not alone anymore,

you are in me,

as water for a pond gold fish,

and a sea breeze for the gull.

You are in my vicinity,

I call upon you,

I know you are there.

You are my blue heart.

I CAN'T STOP

I can't stop the time,

even stop my mind,

wander around the time.

I can't stop the wind,

nor destroy twigs.

I can't stop the rain,

to go against the grain.

I can't stop the night,

to have the last light.

I can't stop the *heart*

beating without your part.

RAINBOW

You were my rain

I wanted to dance under your shower,

You were my rainbow

I wanted to reach the sky with you,

You were my life

I wanted to start again,

You were my red rose

with the fragrance of heaven,

I wanted to pick you up

the thorn hurt my finger.

I woke up

It was a distant rainbow

Grey beneath the grey dream.

DREAM

I dream of *you*, I feel *you,*

an ice block amidst the glimmering fire.

I dream of *you*, I feel *you,*

the scent of my memory.

I dream of *you,* I feel *you*,

the spark of my dark night.

I dream of *you*, I feel *you,*

the beauty of my child-life.

Wait for me I will unite.

LOST

The scar of your dagger on my heart,

That's why I cannot forget your part.

MOTHER EARTH

Why am I lost?

Enkindle the spark of LOVE

in the melody of a disturbed deserted land,

in a searching eyes with blank mind,

in a heart tied to me,

with a flicker of hope to be.

In the bewildering night,

where there is no light.

MOTHER EARTH,

embrace me in your warmth.

To whom can I trust?

I AM REALLY LOST.

STONE

I enjoy being a stone,

in the arms of the field

silent both day and night

ignorant and senseless.

I enjoy being a stone,

not even knowing that.

I don't know since,

when I don't know,

I don't suffer.

When I know that I don't know

I suffer a lot.

I wish I were a stone

in the arms of a field,

clenched in a wall,

pressed into a road,

silent and ignorant.

TO MY MOTHER

To my mother, who is not here to read these lines and I cannot make her happy anymore. Still, there is a pain in my heart to be filled by her kisses.

God gave you a tear to shed,

a tear invisible to me.

I could never ever appreciate you,

who had no dreams, except me.

You were a pillow for my fall,

A ladder for my rise.

To me you were the smile of the sunshine.

Oh mother! a mother still needs you.

YOUR STAR

Being alone at night,

I was too close to the stars.

I could pick the one that I liked!

I raised my head

impressed by those twinklings

let out a very deep sigh,

OOOOOOhhhhh,

which one is your star?

I want to be with you.

A MOTHER

To all innocent children who does not have any body except mother

A mother is not an angel,

there are sometimes when

she is not thinking about her child,

there are some moments when

she cannot remember her child's smile,

and some seconds when

she forgets her child is crying.

A mother is not an angel,

she may be in dream

but not her child's dream.

ME AND I

I send a gift to myself for myself,

to feel that somebody remembers me.

When my pillow is tear-wet,

I wipe my weeping on my cheeks,

to show that somebody is with me.

I smile in front of the mirror,

to share my sweet moments

and lean on a wall,

to sense that if one day I am down,

somebody is near me.

I speak to myself,

cry for myself,

smile with myself.

SMILE

This soul, this heart is wearily worn,

a simple smile could make me happy,

a shallow smile not from the bottom of heart.

A yellow rose could make me glad,

not a bunch of red roses.

A small message, just some simple words,

could make me happy.

This soul, this heart is deprived of the cure needed.

Loneliness is my friend

Loneliness is my close friend,

when with me,

I need nobody.

Loneliness is mine, loneliness is me,

it is always with me,

I do not even feel alone with loneliness beside me.

WINDOW

I will always keep the windows open

to invite you.

If you pass in the street,

I will put the flowers outside

just to smell your fragrance.

If you come

I will switch all the lights off

to see your light

or, no

I will turn on the lights

to observe you better.

Gaze along the street,

my windows are always open

to invite you in.

If one day you should

pass along my street

come out into the open,

into the clearing.

KITE

A colourful kite
my dreams went up to the sky,
up and up and up
to hit the sun.
I took its tread to the wind
the kite escaped to destiny,
the child wept for his lost kite
I cried for my dreams.

AT LEAST A...

A window to happiness,

A wing to highness,

A sun for light,

A star for shine,

A drop of rain for joy,

A day,

A night,

A life,

A death,

A pill to kill

and,

A heart to beat,

once for one.

CAGE

No rose, no garden
no freedom, no sky
no light, no happiness.
I will leave all,
return to you,
return to the cage.
To rose and garden
to freedom and sky
to light and happiness.

BROKEN MEMORIES

Your memory is a treasure

in the safe of my heart.

It is a holy book

and every day I read,

the good scenes of the past;

you and me together

no one else, never.

The book is with me forever.

IT IS BEAUTIFUL

It is beautiful

to wake up at midnight

find it rainy.

You cry unconsciously

for somebody missing.

Somebody near and far

and you do not know where.

It is beautiful

to write for somebody

without any response,

or speak with somebody

without any voice.

It is beautiful

to remember someone,

but no one remembers you.

You cry for somebody,

and no one cries for you.

It is beautiful

to wake up at night

see a shooting star,

and wish,

then tomorrow

you see somebody you love!

HOME

To all women who suffer silently at their own home!

Inside dark, outside dark

no one is waiting for you,

you are waiting for no body

where is home?

A four-wall house to be kept alone,

a place to hide your tears

or if it comes unconsciously,

no one asks why.

Somewhere to veil your heart

and if you want to open it,

no one is there

(although there are some!)

Where is home?

Where no one understands

and live just with each other

but not for each other.

Where is home?

If it is home, then home is home

and everywhere is better than home!

THE SKY AND I MISSED YOU

It was neither winter

nor cold.

Lack of freshness,

The sky burst into tears

I am sure,

The sky and I missed you.

Under the rain

Under the rain, you called me.

Under the rain, you hold me.

Under the rain, you told me.

Under the rain, you left me.

I am waiting for the rain,

For that day again,

To see you, to call you,

to hold you and to tell you.

Friendship

Dr Azadeh Nemati

FRIENDSHIP

Open the window

invite breeze to your party

the sun beam and

the music of chirping birds.

Let candle's flame and breeze be friend.

open the window…

40

REALITY

Mountains stand for ever,

rivers sleep,

yet,

moving.

There is no agony in standing hills,

and no happiness in flowing rivers,

even no pain in sticking stones.

What is hidden in passing these days?

Reality is here, near,

rainbow is a dream

in the night of cactus,

and rain is a strange word,

in the day of desert.

This is reality, near, here!

LIFE

Life is real fantasy

when you are in the boat of love

with oars of dream.

Life is real bliss

when is up with flush of sea

and down with a broken heart,

a defeated soul that can't sing any more.

Life is real fantasy

if you are with me in the voyage

to sing together,

"Life is real bliss,

Life is real fantasy."

BLOSSOM

To blossom, I need fresh air.

To rise, I need a hand.

A warm hand to hold,

A reason to blossom.

My inner bud is blooming,

God! help me, I am glooming.

Send me a warm hand, a reason, and fresh air.

PHOENIX

Plants grow from plants,

Animals breed animals,

Birds hatch.

Idea gives birth to idea.

Poverty brings poverty,

Wealth is the mother of wealth.

Love makes Love,

And hatred are children of hatred.

I rise from ashes.

When burning is complete,

And no corpse is left,

I am the new born phoenix.

NO HOME

We live near,

but we are far.

You don't know me,

I know you less.

At least,

let's not break the mirrors,

if we cannot salute love.

Should it be broken,

we cannot make it again.

Dr Azadeh Nemati

APPLE BASKET

With an apple in hand,

and a basket, full of roses in another,

I was waiting for you.

Starry nights arrived, but not you.

Some dreary times passed,

Sparrows migrated,

Amber blossoms faded,

Gold fish froze,

and rivers dried.

Starry nights arrived, but not you.

I am still waiting,

with the fragrance of apple in hand,

and an empty basket on the other.

Starry nights arrived, but not you.

RESURRECTION

All is darkness,

and the statues' glimpse,

stone statues without heart.

Crows sit on top,

cruelty, multi-foliaged Tulsi,

and no one asked why,

but,

I have never walked on the wet meadow after the rain.

Earth is greedy,

it sucks and hides in its citadels.

The old Guru in the ashram promised:

One day, after the rain,

in the sun rise,

when the sky is cloudy and sunny,

all in the heart of the earth will grow.

One day far, but not near.

OF ANGELS AND DEMONS

Standing lonely in the middle of darkness,

past is gone, future unseen.

I heard the whisper of angels and demons.

Walking slowly near the ocean edge,

the waves yelling and beating my ankles.

Clouds closed the stars' eyes

and no wind could defeat the stingy sky.

No hope to take you out,

no hands to pull you in,

neither the deep ocean,

nor the earth's surface.

Who sings where love is?

Who knows where hope is?

Who shows where light is?

TRUTH

Why all these days are in a hurry to pass??

I can see the moon from balcony.

All the lights are visible in darkness as bright dots.

Stars are not heroes.

If they are true

ask them to shine at noon

in front of the sun.

GONE ARE THE DAYS

Gone are the days.

Not the memories,

which will linger in our heart

for ever, and ever and ever.

Gone are the days.

Still there are lot more,

to come in our life.

No matter how busy you are,

do not forget to live the life that still exists.

I AM WITH YOU

You hear all my stories,

You sitting there silently.

You see all tears rolling on my face,

and a fading smile.

As I am there, you are there,

sitting in the mirror,

on a broken wall.

I am with you,

You on the mirror.

You know my story!

BIRTHDAY OF A STAR

I am invited to the birthday of a star,

tonight in the sky.

I have a pocket of light to bestow

then, tomorrow,

you can see a new smile in the sky.

The youngest smile

can you find?

DROP OF DEW

let me pluck no Daffodil again,

for the romance of

that drop of dew.

Let them be in love,

since they don't know

their moment is brief,

their life is mortal.

Leave them in glory,

in the gleaming eyes

and opened arms.

I WILL PLANT MY HEART

My sliced heart and I were walking under the rain,

I will plant my heart and dance slowly,

under the rain slapping on the ground.

Time is short,

one day in a spring morning it will blossom,

blossoms of a lonely heart.

The music won't last,

I will run through each day,

and fly to the day,

when I plant my heart in rain.

Chanting in my heart:

"every one for himself, God for us all"

I dance slowly under the rain.

SHADOWS

Dance of dark shadows on the ground,

once tall, once short,

sometimes lagging back,

sometimes running in front.

I am with my shadow,

still standing in the darkness,

tired of shadows,

I wanna salute the sun!

IF IT IS TRUE LOVE...

If it is true,

it sparkles for ever,

it blossoms at any time,

and gives birth to the new stars and spring buds.

If it is true,

it never fades with a gentle blow

it never pales with other colours.

No one can steal it,

even no body can touch it,

it will never die in our heart,

if it is a true Love.

CHILDHOOD DREAM

How happy childhood world is,

full of green emotions.

A child is happy

with a light, colourful balloon

throwing ups and down.

A child is happy

with a piece of brown chocolate,

it is enough to change the taste of his mouth,

How sweet his life is!

LOVE

I love darkness,

because in darkness I see light,

I love night,

at night I have moon,

I love sadness,

to search for happiness,

I love brown soil,

where red rose and green leaves grow,

I love ocean,

source of motion,

I love you,

to live without you.

SEA IS NOT GENEROUS

sea is generous

everybody says,

full of water, vast and open:

it is not generous

for a thirsty man

looking for a drop of water.

BEAUTIFUL MOMENTS

I wanted to share
my beautiful moments
with you.
When you left,
beautiful moments
left without trace.
Come,
I am waiting to share
my sweet moments with you.

GLOOMY TWILIGHT

The scene of a gloomy twilight,

Dark with some birds lost,

Still all the sands and dust,

With a bird on top of tall tree,

Chirping in a lovely sound,

is the heart-renting tale

of a whirling ghost.

LONELY HEART

hand in hand

we could feel the coldness of sand,

we were making footprints behind

and the waves destroyed.

In front of the yelling sea,

and the fallen sun

you told me,

I read your poems,

I live you, I love you.

but you have never asked

why "lonely heart" !

www.ingramcontent.com/pod-product-compliance
Lightning Source LLC
Chambersburg PA
CBHW070058100426
42740CB00013B/2868